standing in the flock of connections

standing in the flock of
connections

Heather Cadsby

Brick Books

Library and Archives Canada Cataloguing in Publication

Cadsby, Heather, author
    Standing in the flock of connections / Heather Cadsby.

Poems.
Issued in print and electronic formats.
ISBN 978-1-77131-479-4 (softcover).—ISBN 978-1-77131-481-7 (PDF).—
ISBN 978-1-77131-480-0 (EPUB)

    I. Title.

PS8555.A27S73 2018   C811'.54   C2017-907247-1
                                               C2017-907248-X

We acknowledge the Government of Canada, the Canada Council for the Arts, and the Ontario Arts Council for their support of our publishing program.

The author photograph was taken by Rebecca Pedoe.
Cover image: "Mirroring," by Marvyne Jenoff, photography collage on paper.
The book is set in Scalal.
Design and layout by Marijke Friesen.
Printed and bound by Sunville Printco Inc.

Brick Books
431 Boler Road, Box 20081
London, Ontario N6K 4G6

www.brickbooks.ca

For
Theodore Russell Cadsby
Jana Meredith Cadsby Bell

Contents

Text steps

Behind my back someone stole a bunch of words

Our shadows were moving ahead of us

Who is butterfly?

I've never clasped my name
the way a monarch does.
Or been named after.

This insect with no backbone
resembles me in other ways.
I have laid four hundred eggs in the past.

Two fertilized.
I was smaller than my mate,
found glory in the morning

with my many body parts
and sore shoulders.
I was jealous of wings

that flew her into my house
to steal my milk (myth #1).
(She tastes bad to some.)

Seeing her moving in a gang
meant imminent war (myth #2).
In the Middle Ages, people didn't fly.

At stages of belly stretch
I said she sheds so easily.
Layers discarded. I'm fussing.

We all have our little commotions,
finding a bite to eat,
a straw for drinking.

Waxmakers and masons

They do it all, these women
who've been nurses and fanners.
In divisions of labour, they've done every job,
are perfectly suited to votes and decisions.

They have no quarrel with the few gorgeous men
who can't take the winters here.
They are soon dead and left
in a pile at the door.

No hour is wasted. Each gesture heroic.
A figure-eight skater describes a nectar source
or a possible new home
if the din gets too much.

Then it's the old royal lady who leaves
with some waiters and maids.
A young beauty inherits the castle
and the beebread.

Steadfast and steady,
her workers begin to specialize
in the unbroken arrangement
that is older than reptiles.

Eats fish and small birds

From Van Dusen footbridge
I look down at Mimico Creek.
A mink is crossing
back and forth, east to west to east.
Scrambles up the bank
into one rock notch
and out of another,
flies down into water again,
head popping in and out of sight
like a plane passing in and out of clouds.

A raucous duck caw
cracks the silence,
announces a family paddling upstream.
Eight ducklings herded by parents
defeating the mink's darting ways.
No successful dinner grab
as the drake, bringing up the rear,
blasts a trumpet-tongued honking squawk
like no duck I've ever heard.

Gestures simply slip out and on

Turtles are very old, have no teeth.
Not lost, never had. Not fearful

of first-person singular.
No turtle turmoil. A reptilian gaze

is fixed on us as you
adjust the focus.

This is our assignment. A singular adventure
to create a life list for ourselves.

Something outside ourselves. Before
we do ourselves in. Copulation

requires an hour under water.
Aye aye aye.

But we're off to a good start.
So get your picture.

We'll call this one *painted*
and turn the page

as if that's all we need
to know it all.

Stroke

Our shadows were moving
ahead of us. In high spirits
we began a morning walk. Talk
of blue manicures, ladybugs
in ceiling fixtures.

She said her face was tingling.
She laughed and we both
launched into extremes. Aha—
tingling like rapid-fire piano scales,
like a face in a lawn sprinkler,
like holding a royal flush,
like shoplifting eyeshadows.

What we didn't say
was next destination.
Alienating word reverberating
in cold corridor, blankets, sudden hours
until a machine confirms the truth. And you
bury your hand in bedding
so it won't flip up, whack your face.

Those painted nails, running metaphors,
winged things.

One of those periods of audit

There's something I'd rather be doing.
A few minutes ago I knew what it was
but now it's gone. Maybe I'm in the midst of it.
Likely that's it. Time flies
when you're spinning wheels. He turned
a game show into a piece of art.
I'd like to thank maths, physics, and chemistry
and Gabriel Fauré and my grandfather's clause.
His clock was a piece of work, I tell you,
always singing on one brutal note.
Time to rephotograph and reassess
before the dealers come on strong with their lowballs.

There's something I was meant to achieve.
It was a goal that I lost
and you didn't win.
Was it rushing to a grave? I need the exact number
of minutes for that idea to take hold. You said
you were afraid of yourself. I think
that is some sort of sham excuse.
Like: *Sorry he's in a meeting at the moment.*
Like: *Sorry she can't talk now.*
I'm sitting sad on the time-out spot.
Moving clocks run slow.
There's just this: sleep and hurry.

This morning, starting out

My mind is racing.
I've asked to be alone. I need natural things
like toddlers on the telephone,
like old men walking rhythmically with canes.

There is my apartment and there is the whole building.
I need the ratio.
Light on the balcony is interrupted daily.
It never makes it to the west wall.
I mention this a lot. I mention birds
and birds hitting windows.
Mention cooking odours and weather and shopping.
Reasons why I've asked to be alone.

Once when I was talking on the phone to my mother
I was flipping through the newspaper.
Did she hear this?
She asked to speak to her grandchild.
And later she asked me to help her. I said, Uh huh.

This morning I feel intended for violence.
I am this big.

Between love and death

The men are showing off,
whooping and running around
the playing field
shadow-boxing, air-guitaring,
wrestling their sons to the ground.

Swing from the trees, my darlings.
You know it's better with friends.
Easier to impress if you've forgotten how.
Where did your wives go, my dears?

The men with kids are left
no longer cocky, reverting to frantic
and all this cavorting
with glances at the beautiful woman
reading in the afternoon sun.
Her purple floppy hat protects her story:
her tragedies, her nostalgia, her griefs.

And now, dear men,
it's time to calm down. Your kids
are hungry. The game is over.
The beautiful woman
will return as a fantasy.

How Love Works. What Sex Means

Doing, a filthy pleasure is, and short ...
—*Gaius Petronius (c. 27 AD – 66 AD)*
(trans. Ben Jonson)

There is a great deal of unmapped country within us which would have
to be taken into account in an explanation of our gusts and storms.
—*George Eliot (1819 – 1880)*

In the beginning

For his birthday
she knitted a pair of white wool socks.
First time
with four needles and necessary skills:

> ribbing the cuff
> turning the heel
> picking up gussets
> closing the toe

Her mother
teaching it all so patient and proud.

She thinks he liked them.

But they got into an accident.
His mother
shrunk them in the washing machine.

For a minute

In the middle of changing my mind
I changed my mind.
It wasn't a yes/no thing,
more like a love. Say
everything we do is love, so if
I'm always sad about my mother
or stroke the restless legs
that jerk me wide awake, it's all
just curse and bless.
Don't blame your legs or
the ice eyes of your mother.
Neurologists say it's all
in your brain, so if
your mirror neurons are plentiful
you're likely in my shoes already,
which makes us really all of one mind.

One another

The one: No love without sex.
The other: No sex without desire.
The one: Gentle ideas. Brutal imaginings.
The other: Ear to chest: Liar Liar.
The one: Bodily clamour.
The other: I bend you to my will.
The one: With force. With neglect, that bitter pill.
The other: With bend-over pleasure skill.

My account of the carjacking is fictional

I used it as a way of getting to you.
Same with the mermaid toy. I knew with you
there were no unspeakable vices.
No sitting slumped in guilt.
And sure enough
what you did with that Mercedes hood ornament
I can only call a scherzo of sweetness
wonders and dangers
that gets found and lost and found.
The loneliest of feasts.

When I switched back to glasses from contacts
those tiny things were a night's worth of questioning.
Why why why and how do I
fit *libido dominandi* into a real poem.

Mentionables

Rope, fly swatter, old telephone, baster, ratchet tie-down,
boxing glove, satin teddy, piss shoe, garden paraphernalia,
rings, plugs, vibes, beads, *The Garden of Earthly Delights* (centre panel).

    Delight in sex when it comes my way.
    Love you best from far away.

See us messing around with our props and potentials.
A frozen freedom to be this uninvolved and constantly inventing.

The time between

The thing about getting back together
is what was removed and then lost
when the door closed. That time
when singular things happened
and we didn't know we were waiting.
It's not a question of emptiness
even though something was taken out
of the earlier time.
And now we attempt to put it back in
and say, Looks just like before. But
something isn't matching up,
isn't holding its own,
is only running parallel to hoping.
Questions arise.
We answer like doubles of ourselves.
Or I'm still original but you aren't.
Or everyone is always separate
and how do we live from a beginning again
emptying our pockets on the dresser.
Coming clean is as good as it gets
without describing the contents
with built-in sadness.

Let me tell you where I've been

instead of here with you.

It was exciting imagining
those shrieking sisters watching.

I can't use glue or screws, preheat or bend
anything today.

We will always
be more curious than tomorrow.

Yes absolutely
put on that gardening smock.

And like conflicted protagonists in isolation
let's grow the similes slowly.

8th floor lookout

We were struggling to expand
a compromise, when we lost sight
of the issue. The context shifted.
We returned to solitary parallel
observations out the window. I saw
a hawk land in a tree crotch
and spread its wings for balance.
In its talons a frenzy
of thrashing squirrel. With woodpecker
speed the hawk pecked at its head,
going for brain, the delicacy.
On the ground below
no shadow was cast,
a couple walked by,
some boys played grabnuts,
a car was parking. Too much to see
as the hawk with prey took off. I was alone
looking at us casting first stones,
and it wasn't over yet.

Dragging our dreams and damages into everything

Stripped of imagination
it is simply skin rubbing skin.
And a little story like
hurry hurry
or *not allowed to pee*
or *broken legs can't run*
or *pry open your mother.*

Nothing beyond a road to get there.
Any imagined justice gets stripped.
We were asking for it.
We made the face
that's meant to make us think
all yours or *anything you'd like to try.*

My turn to turn away.
But only as a mind
which still attaches a story of perhaps.

Remember when you said that thing

The third wish is about listening
and thinking about listening.
Watch me thinking. That's love
if you can manage it.

You suggest sunglasses are blocking my thoughts.
I say you are not listening.
There's no bruise to hide here.

We've been through the new clothes,
the old standards, jazz paintings, billiards, half-hearted cleanups.
I love these. All this nicey-nicey.

And what was I thinking doing that
while you were listening to yourself.
Also a broken heart and where it hurts exactly
when you're thinking about it.

I am the better listener. I pay for it
in cash, in fiction, in feedbacks.
You have the beach and boardwalk butt.
I have the happy hair.

So, we got the first two wishes out of the way.
That counts for something.
Yay us. We did it. You say,
Do it do it do it.

A stiletto removed

Offered up, sniffed, stroked,
placed sideways on the bed. Red red rose.

Face-to-face, unfenced, silent.
The result never long enough.

In the end, at the end, begin again.

What do we do now?
We wait. It's boring.
Boredom is the wish for desire.
And the grudge at the root of it all.

      Why do you say blow when you mean suck?
      And this is not my vagina.

          Whatever, I like it stubbled. This shaver head will work.
          Yes. Perfect.

That pile is beautiful.
I'm so auburn. We should save it.

Age-old question

Someone is following me.
It's a man with thin legs.
He drives behind me on the 401.
He walks just off to my left
on the St. Lawrence boardwalk.
He sits in a booth at my local pub
watching me recover.
One day I thought he'd left me
when I saw him stumble-running, drunk-on
after another woman.
She didn't want sex, he told me.
He told me most of them aren't horny anymore.
What about me? I asked.
You baby, he rasped, need to stay sober.
Two drunks can really fuck up the whole roll.

I tell myself he is watching me.
It's too upsetting to think he'll do nothing.

Like in an occupied city, you are there

What I see
I'll never see again.

A slightly crooked painting
righted by your restless hand.

Hands clasped behind your head.
Your moving mind.

What I heard were fantastic delusions.
Your naked self.

Meds to keep you clean.
Take away the mean.

What caught your eye. Specks
anywhere, commonplace, buzzing you crazy.

You pretending to sleep. Me
pretending everything. Shame

to fool you like this/that.
What do I know? Maybe you

do know. Did you?
My wish was always if.

Going mad, seeing eyes

This is about everything that was taken.
What he was given in return was a pack of lies.
Syllables of debris, an exploded view.
Something crashed into his brain
at the love site. Something fiery and black.
A hole filled with delusions.

> *She is running a sex service.*
> *She has to have her vagina filled six times a day.*
> *She buys men drinks, brings them home.*
> *She was on a cruise ship, with a boy in the berth.*
> *She fucks my brother.*
> *Once on the phone, her voice was hoarse. Proof.*
>
> *She lies when she denies everything.*

The lies are his. They are fantasies of a broken brain.

Most days he sits quiet. A man in a bathrobe.
He has reeled everything in.

Hitting the Golden Ratio once in a while

Sunday geometer

When you're all thumbs
the Fermi rule is a comforting thing.
If you can't actually count
every hair on your arm
you can get solace from the master of estimation.
Better to be approximately right
than precisely wrong.
Hitting the Golden Ratio once in a while
can open your eyes for tomorrow.
Speculation ongoing. Degradation eroded.
You could wait all year for the calendrical cognate of pi
or say it's someone's birthday today.

I love a pentagram. You can draw that thing
all day freehand, sloppy. Five-star
hotels, movies, generals. Throw it around
like it was a love number, which it is.
Cut an apple horizontally, there it is.
Draw one inside its centre pentagon and so on
nesting smaller forever. Till you call it quits
and start singing Holy, etc.

The whole play consists of stage directions

Are we waiting out the storm
or is the storm wearing us out?
The usual standstill moments.
Looks like you've turned your back to me.
There's a sheet of rain between us
and I've turned my back to you which,
in this blurry landscape and
assuming a squint and an eye-in-the-sky perspective,
could be bilateral symmetry except
for the differences which fascinate.
Is the tiny shiver a chill or love?

Looking around for some good old solid things.
I'm bored trying to make pentagonal paper bookmarks.
I don't even get it. And someone (was it you?)
stepped on my cream-coloured tetrahedron.
I can behave all hard done by,
which is at least something enjoyable.

And as if in apology, you lend me some crystals.
I accept our small selfish pursuits.
You want me to stick around. I need something amiss.

Hot talk. Not really

The conversations range in all directions.
Now anything is fair game.
If visual perception in monkeys
and circumference/diameter ratio are meaningful,
so are comments on oatmeal cookies
and nasty digs about upstarts.
Raspberry pi is a thing now. This credit-card-size computer.
Much of the cortex is plastic.
Non-stop creativity.
Real estate can change hands. Relocated.
Born blind? Visual cortex gets used for other stuff.
Environments are open houses.
The sex of sea turtles is determined by environment temperatures.
Everyone listens to hip hop. No they don't.

I found a window

Hung it on a wall.
It is better than a mirror
because you can see to the other side.
I moved it
to hang over my grandmother. I mean
the portrait of my grandmother.
She is three years old in the painting.
I never knew her
to look like that.
But now with the window over her
it has become a sweet Victorian style
portrait of a rosy-cheeked child.
Beautiful, now I don't have to
get all sentimental about my family.

Tomorrow I will move the window over
to cover my mother's snowshoes,
which I've also hung on my wall.
They were hers when she was a child.
They always make me sad
because the little straps
for her little boots
are still there and all frayed.
I cry because I never knew her
when she clomped through snow
on these small things.
But tomorrow they will be
under a window,
fine Edwardian artifacts.

Aubade

The crack of dawn
sound I missed.
I did not know the first light
was to be the last you would see.
It would be your death day.
I was elsewhere remembering
you bending down each morning
tying my shoes.
It seemed unlived-through,
this daily gesture
that took three or four years.
It was during the war
but not an urgent time for us.
We were Canadian people.

Out the hospital window I saw a dove. It was a gull

Get up. Get going.
I got up and went to see my mother.
She was very old and dying.

Turn left at the first hallway.
I turned left and found my mother.
She was dead with her mouth open.

A beautiful nurse said,
Here's tea. We're sorry.
We've called your sister. Take your time.
I'm sure she loved you.

I tried to climb into bed with her.
I wanted to crush her.
She was already dead. Help me.

Cover her up, Heather.
My sister knew my craziness. She pulled
the sheet over the gaping mouth,
the slightly open eyes.

Ha ha you girls missed the show.
I saw her pee pee.
The gleeful woman in the bed across the room
saw removal of the catheter, bag of urine.

My mother loved to show off.
When do you stop knowing
someone's looking at you.

Handwork accompaniment

Those who push plastic tabs into sockets.
Those who repeatedly say *no don't touch.*
Those who can't be bothered keeping
an eye on everything.
Know they could miss things.
Know the need for connection.

I will stroke her as soon as
she is released from my body.
I will cut bait with a baby gate.

The little ones keep on going
crawling their way to praiseworthy obsession.
Good job. We master the set-up steps for pack 'n play.
Those who hang wallpaper plumb-lined perpendicular.
Those who slap it up in time for drinks.
The edge remains regardless of ritual.
A notch on the belt, height-mark on the doorframe.
Tap-test the mic and we're good to go.

Three miscarriages and my daughter is pregnant again

Another unexpected guest has started the journey
hot on the heels
of the recently departed.
We are a friendly family.
We will do our best to welcome you.
We say sorry
if we seem exhausted.
It's just that we barely had time to catch our breath.
The three before you changed their minds
and left abruptly. Each departure
enlarged our sadness, slowed our hope
until now we fear the worst:

Your jaw will jut beyond
the possibility of speech.
Your eyes will bulge out to see
what the blind know.
Your forehead will rise
uncontrollably, like dough.

The language of grief is the language of hope.
To speak it, we breathe. For now
you are the breath of the world
wandering around mountains.

Spectrum

The problem with a broken brain
is every would-be fix goes upper limits.
You think you've got it solved and then
things start to rattle like before.

We need to slow him down, she says.
Pills, I think, should do the trick.
They do for months, nearly a year
until depression claims the stage.

A change of meds brings on new hope,
skyrocketing dreams, and mother's prayer.
They work for the preteen phase.
Then he plummets, stays locked in bed,

and once again she plans for him.
Tutors, gym passes, part-time jobs.
He's now a teen, her choices lost.
Weed, booze, knives, guns

have made it clear that nothing's clear
except he's left.
She looks at laundry,
goes back to bed.

My Michael (1996–2009)

Clumped loam in snow beside the winter weeds.
Brittle brown and broken-backed as no
Summer swaying selves, alive with seeds,
Expected this, in time, the way to go.

I watch you on the dirt bike learning how
To stop and start and turn the thing around.
A careful boy who half a year from now
Is body struck, left dying on the ground.

I drink too much. My diet's full of fat.
The noon crow and my phone seem set in sync.
I live in woods, our whole life used to that.
Consider silence as the missing link.

A single mother never anymore.
Just single now, still listening by the door.

My you is dead

The last breath opened your eyes. I see you not seeing. I am denied the speaking object, the last resort of the speaking subject. The power of questioning is foreclosed. I read something and I am furious. It doesn't mention my only referent. What do I care about pasta or kaleidoscopes? Ultimately I have to belittle to get my teeth brushed. You could be a real asshole. Rinse, swish, spit. Because what is laid on by protocol, and intended to confirm, is doomed by well-meaning. I am witness to a desperate resistance within me. My only recourse is a forced exit from critical language, so I can try to formulate the fundamental feature. Door opens. Hi there I'm home. Only your ball cap on the hook still. I have whacked it on and off a million times. I have lost the language of love. The give and take of it. Alone, disarmed, composed, there is one credit. A lightness.

Text steps

Beware of speaking of sayings as if they were closed

If a bird in the hand is worth two in the bush, what time is it? It should be early enough to get a worm or two. Early birds can then sing their hearts out. We deserve that. Nothing like sunrise birdsong to lift the spirits. A veery is one example. If you place seeds in your outstretched hand, it's likely a chickadee will land. This can become boring and lead you to believe a birdwalk in the woods is better. Even if the woods are lovely dark, there's no guarantee you'll spot a rarity. You'll likely emerge eyes empty of birds, shoes mud-caked, and hair damp if it's early in the morning. Quite an experience, you say if you're an optimist. Which is a problem because that attitude makes you lose track of the project. A project is a cultural experience. As they say in Latin, *Certa amittimus dum incerta petimus*. Something about certainty.

Beware of speaking of the others as if they were someone else

If you are left to stew in your own juice, does your mind narrow to a trench, walled by the original miserable mistake? Do you remain entrenched in your mealy-mouthed convolutions, still claiming hearty robust recipe status? A proverbial pot among hissing kettles? And if your juice is formaldehyde, a better story forms. You are a deformed syllable waiting for clarity in stasis. And in some narrow-minded liner note, a pact with facts was made. You are left still in status-seeking conclusions. Not your own.

Beware of speaking of the winners as if they were someone else

If a miss is as good as a mile, and I lose by an inch and it's been replayed and recounted and reconfirmed a close second, am I nothing? Even though I gave the winner an inch? There is no such thing as almost won, almost scored. In fact it is a mile-high ego that is strutting around, trophy raised, notch on the belt. OK. You scored. Wherever. Lots of times. Lucky for you, this girl don't stay for breakfast.

Beware of speaking of the followers as if they were someone else

If a stitch in time saves nine, why are the nine ladies dancing? Did they slack off or was one of them speedier at the sampler? A conscientious girl with a bag of threads on her arm who may have been kicked out of the group because her timing was off. Choreography depends on synchronization. If you lag behind the beat, you're out. Even if you plead syncopation. Improv isn't respected in a chorus line. Or on starter embroidery projects.

Beware of speaking of the avengers as if they were someone else

If you're gonna wash that man right outta your hair, do you need to bother about applying conditioner afterwards? Your fabulous sigh of relief may have left it gleaming. But if it looks like something's missing, you could try WD-40. You'd get a nice glow as well as defrizzing, and it wouldn't rust in the rain. On the other hand, if your relief turns to revenge, you can always go at it with scissors. And pretend it's his.

Beware of speaking of the rich as if they were someone else

In order to have your cake and eat it too, do you have to be ambidextrous? Have a conjoined twin? Or hold stock in a gold mine and wear a gold ring? What about crumbs? Are they considered having or eating? And you'd need to tread carefully if you have allergies. You could have a piece of someone's homemade from scratch. But if you actually eat it, well, you should keep in mind your last midnight trip to the ER. But manners dictate no refusals. Acceptance is the rule. So unless you are one of those grande dames with poodles and jewels, you'd best stuff it in your purse and high-five the host.

Beware of speaking of the generalists as if they were someone else

If you are a jack of all trades and master of none be expansive with your projects. Let boredom dictate their abandonment. Be serious and refuse contention. Let adversaries dissolve in your kindness. Be a daily reader of blogs. Let dabbling be your way. Be without genius. Let others break through the lines. Be always late. Let others assume that lateness defines you. Be constant in pursuing this and that. Let lack of perseverance be your song of songs.

Beware of speaking of the sleepers as if they were someone else

If you sleep like a log, are you stuck in a forest for a hundred years? How many zees make up a century? All your sheep would be dead and your hair would be beyond bed. You'd need a huge dose of nostalgia to get going again. The danger is you might actually become a log. In which case you'd be forever destined to helping little ones with their fear of falling asleep. My advice is to get up, drink warm milk, and check your messages.

Behind my back someone
stole a bunch of words

Your prose poem, she said

Too story. Too attempting. Homeostatic when it should be catawampus. The *spiny softshell turtle* is interesting. But *its head went in and out?* Your piece needs a couple of nihilistic gestures. *I crept up on a loved one, stroked and kissed.* OK. But why cross out *she hauled off and punched me?* Extend your imagery. And lineation isn't the convention breaker. Losing a pacing device doesn't eliminate pace. You can be dreamlike, frenzied, chopped, smashed, or meditative. *I dared him, armed with a safety net* is a good start towards destabilizing. You need to cast wider. Defeat my expectation. Deny me passivity. Keep at it. Use my mockery. Prose poem is a ludic genre worth some failing.

The cause of my rosacea

We usually get together once a year and pick a fight . . . his messed-up life, my spending habits, stupid haircuts. Sometimes it escalates to re-enactments of historical feuds. This year we were going on about the Debussy/Saint-Saëns spat. I said Camille didn't give me any credit for my innovations. He said Claude was way too disrespectful of his genius. And since we both were calling ourselves poets, we thought we knew a thing or two about creating. When he said that there is no one more avant than himself and that my theory is all rhyme and reason, I said, I'm not enjoying this conversation. And that was when he shouted, This isn't a conversation, it's a prose poem.

There are times when even the thought of a prose poem makes my face raging red.

All these things and what to do with them

A speck, a pinprick, a seed, a cup. Thank you cervical collar and dark chocolate.

A woman used a back-scratcher and thought to write about it. The question wasn't how. The question was why bother.

To be a woman picturing herself far away on a hill. Just a dot on the landscape. No acne, no anger. She is standing in the flock of connections. Nodding in agreement.

To connect the dots you first have to find them. You could start with love if you can imagine such a lopsided thing. A biff on the head, a kick in the pants, a kiss on the lips. In a certain light you can make everything lovely.

If you clear everything out there will be no squabbling. Goodbye Hummel figurine, lyre table, cobalt miniatures. Accidents don't happen in an empty room. Until you slip on the bare floor and slide on your path to happiness.

It's a blessing, this questioning of gratitude. Now, with everything facing the sunny side, you're ready to exit. With thanks. You're welcome. Everyone's welcome.

Life Drawing: graduating class

These students are nearly finished. Four years of drawing the human body in head-and-shoulders portrait or costume or nude. The instructor says, Let's see some excellent pieces today. One pose. Three hours. Take your time. Walk around the model. Choose your spot thoughtfully.

I am seated on a cube. One foot on a smaller cube. One leg outstretched. One forearm resting on a thigh. Wrist and hand falling loose. Other hand placed firmly on the main cube. Back relaxed. Head turned and tilted. Three hours. Two ten-minute breaks.

During the first break I hear him say, Good stuff. Some really nice work happening. A couple of crackerjack pieces over there. Yours, Kevin. And Jodie's.

Then he says, Some models give something that makes for better art.

During the second break he's really raving about the top-notch quality of today's drawings. I wander around and see creased bellies, sagging breasts, gnarled fingers, jowls. All beautifully rendered.

Artist from Armenia lands in America

What you need to know about Arshile Gorky is that he witnessed so much death he began to think of himself as a murderer. This is not so strange when you think of that identifying-with-your-captor syndrome. So if you bumped into Gorky before 1948 but after, say, 1920 you might rush to get out of his way and jump at the chance to shake his hand. That's the thing about a person like that who's always trying to accumulate details so as to be clear of them. For example, all his name changes. I, for one, would never want to be his mother who was over and over being left for dead. How many times can a person take that? Especially since every time it came up you'd have to raise your peaceful head to reassure your son. I would never want to be his student because I'm the kind of subgenius who wants direction in my drawing and he gets angry when you try to make sense of his commands. And to be his wife you'd have to lure him into bed where he'd bite you in a very unpleasant way and you'd know that was likely all he'd do. Mostly he'd be working on new studies for a self-portrait. The thing about a person like that is the distance between homicides and a suicide.

From Wink Texas. Yes Wink

I had been under the covers crying over Roy Orbison since I had been travelling undercover as Claudette his teen wife till she was killed on her motorcycle and I became the song which had been ruined by the Everly Brothers even though the angelic Roy had written me as the pretty woman and those two squares who couldn't see anything beyond their rights were no three-octave-Ravel appreciators like my operatic rocker that love so beautiful that standstill candyman with bad eyes and dyed hair and a heart that didn't last past crying it's over. I had been crying over my bolero man.

Sometimes how it goes

I had just finished writing one of my better poems so I decided to brush off cookie crumbs and give it a little shake. I noticed that some words had lost letters. Also lots of punctuation had fallen out and a few line breaks changed direction. Not so bad, really. I could use fewer commas, and line breaks are notoriously personal. I wasn't worried as I gave it a sweep with my hand to make sure it was a clean copy. That was when some typos flew off the page. Good thing. You don't want one of your better poems marred by typos. Then as I was picking up these flakes, behind my back someone stole a bunch of words. I'm not sure about this, but certainly a lot of spaces appeared. And as I was trying to hold onto the few words that were left, I saw that they weren't even mine. . . . *had he lived, Humpty Dumpty might have been a mother.* . . . Thank you Russell Edson.

Do those flowers on the wall look dead to you?

When the therapist asked what exactly I was afraid of, I told him boredom. Yes, he said, lots of people have a fear of boredom. Very common. I can definitely help you get over that.

No, I said, I don't want to get over it. I'm afraid I will lose it. There are so many forces that endanger it. I feel constantly threatened, and now I see that you too are trying to pry it away from me. My husband has tried to trick me into playing chess with him. My son has placed outlines for Continuing Ed courses on my desk. My sister has suggested nature walks and my best friend invites me to concerts. These conspirators are determined to rob me of my boredom. I am at my wits' end. I spend all this energy fending off cures when I could be enjoying boring times; guarding my secrets and incessant thoughts. I tell you, my supply is dwindling.

The therapist sat up. Ah, so your problem is hoarding. I can easily set you up with a clutter specialist, who will have more expertise. My practice is pretty much limited to interpretation.

Biographemes

If you are the bilingual kid you get to play Santa. You think that's why. If you are the girl with claw hands you are benched in gym class. You walk there. If you are a daughter setting out for church, your little roadside prayers are for removal of budding things. Harbingers of the first season of blood. Out of the blue, a mother says, just like that, sex-ruined. But she didn't say that. She was tongue-tied in all languages. If you are a mother and you go away, you leave a space in your child's mind. It is a place where new memories would have gone if you'd stayed. It is like that even in pleasant towns and productive lives.

What this poem means

It means your California clothes have waltzed across the bridge over
  troubled waters
It means living off your Visa card and the 12-string guitar sounds like
  an orchestra so why not
Earth is restaurant food leftovers in food trucks heading to food hand-
  outs the poor shall inherit
It means a cane wound round with a tensor bandage
On the pulse of morning → On the pumice of morons. We love our
  games
Epicurus, epigenetics: new words from minimal deviation. Same old
  same old
If you think you'll die badly you need to say sorry and bring it on already
Figure 6: the author at age twenty-five or so. Those days these days it
  means this life this mind

Acknowledgements

Some of these poems have appeared in the following publications: *The Antigonish Review, Arc Poetry Magazine, The Dalhousie Review, The Fiddlehead, The New Quarterly, Prairie Fire, PRISM international.*

Earlier versions of some poems in Text steps appeared in a self-published artifact.

I am grateful for the support of the Toronto Arts Council and the Ontario Arts Council.

HEATHER CADSBY was born in Belleville, Ontario and moved to Toronto at a young age. In the 1980s, along with Maria Jacobs, she produced the monthly periodical *Poetry Toronto* and founded the poetry press Wolsak and Wynn. Also at this time, she organized poetry events at the Axle-Tree Coffee House and Phoenix: A Poet's Workshop. In recent years, she has served as a director of the Art Bar Poetry Series. *Standing in the Flock of Connections* is her fifth collection of poetry.